Going Supernova

Space Exploration

Charles Hope

Contents

What's Out There?	2
The Space Age	4
Walking in Space	6
The Apollo Program	8
Man Walks on the Moon	10
Exploring the Moon	12
Space Shuttles	14
Living in Space	16
Rovers and Probes	18
Deep Space	20
Satellite Communication	22

WHAT'S OUT THERE?

Humans have always been fascinated by space. For thousands of years astronomers have looked at the Moon, Sun and stars in an effort to make sense of the universe, and to understand our place within it. Up until the 20th century people looked at space from the ground, using their eyes or with the help of telescopes. That all changed with the beginning of the Space Age.

DID YOU KNOW?

The first telescopes were invented in the Netherlands in 1608. The following year, Galileo Galilei improved on these designs, creating a telescope that could magnify objects up to 20 times.

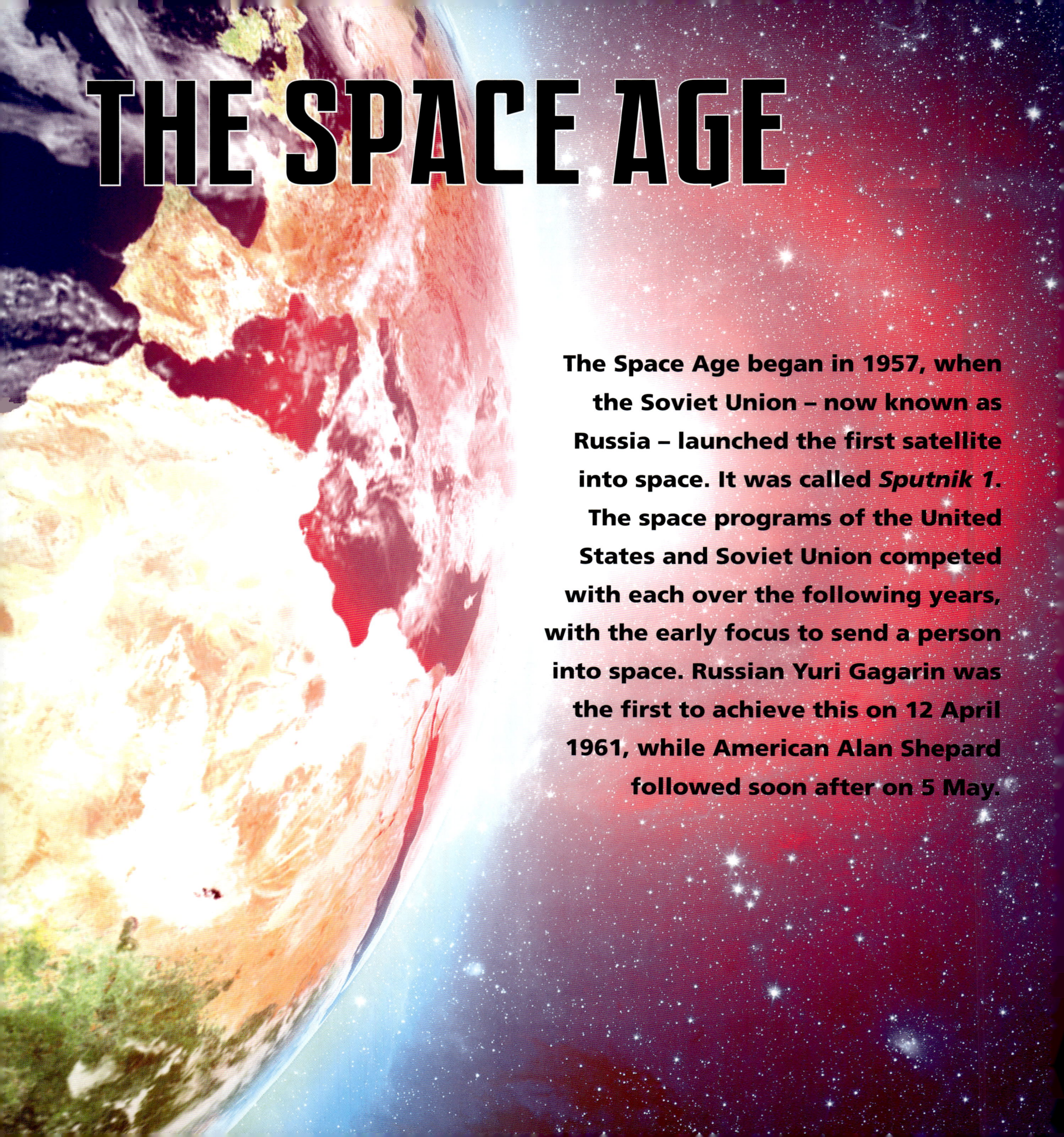

THE SPACE AGE

The Space Age began in 1957, when the Soviet Union – now known as Russia – launched the first satellite into space. It was called *Sputnik 1*. The space programs of the United States and Soviet Union competed with each over the following years, with the early focus to send a person into space. Russian Yuri Gagarin was the first to achieve this on 12 April 1961, while American Alan Shepard followed soon after on 5 May.

DID YOU KNOW?

A wide variety of animals have taken part in space travel, including fruit flies, monkeys, mice, frogs, guinea pigs, chimpanzees and dogs.

WALKING IN SPACE

After it was discovered that people could travel safely into space, one of the next major achievements was extra-vehicular activity, or spacewalking. This involved an astronaut leaving the spacecraft, with the aid of a special suit that was tied to the ship. It was an important breakthrough as it allowed astronauts to make repairs to their ship. Russian cosmonaut Alexey Leonov was the first to perform this amazing feat, on 18 March 1965.

Astronauts can now work in space with the assistance of robotic arms, or with a special piece of equipment that uses jet-thrusters to control movement.

DID YOU KNOW?
The longest spacewalk in history lasted eight hours and 56 minutes. It was performed by astronauts Jim Voss and Susan Helms on 11 March 2001.

THE APOLLO PROGRAM

A major moment in space exploration was landing a person on the Moon. This achievement was made possible by the Apollo program, a NASA project that ran from 1961 to 1972. Along with the Gemini program, it made discoveries that were essential to landing a person on the Moon. These included space rendezvous, when two spacecraft get within visual contact of each other, and space docking, when two spacecraft attach to one another.

DID YOU KNOW?

The command module, the only section of the Apollo spacecraft to return to Earth, is 3 metres high and 4 metres wide. Three people and a lot of equipment had to fit into this cramped space.

MAN WALKS ON THE MOON

The world watched with amazement as Apollo 11 astronauts Neil Armstrong and Edwin "Buzz" Aldrin landed on the Moon, on 20 July 1969. It was the first time a human being had ever set foot on the Moon.

DID YOU KNOW?

This footprint, left by Edwin "Buzz" Aldrin, could remain for as long as the Moon exists. This is because there is no atmosphere on the Moon, and no wind or water to disturb it.

EXPLORING THE MOON

The Apollo program was designed to help scientists learn all they could about the Moon. Astronauts would land the lunar module section of their spacecraft on the Moon's surface, where they performed experiments and collected samples of soil and rock.

Astronauts travelled about on a buggy known as a lunar roving vehicle.

DID YOU KNOW?
Only 12 people have set foot on the Moon.

13

SPACE SHUTTLES

In 1981 came the development of the space shuttle. For the first time a spacecraft could be partially reused, saving space agencies an enormous amount of money. They also helped with important jobs like transporting astronauts and cargo into space, launching satellites and constructing the *International Space Station*.

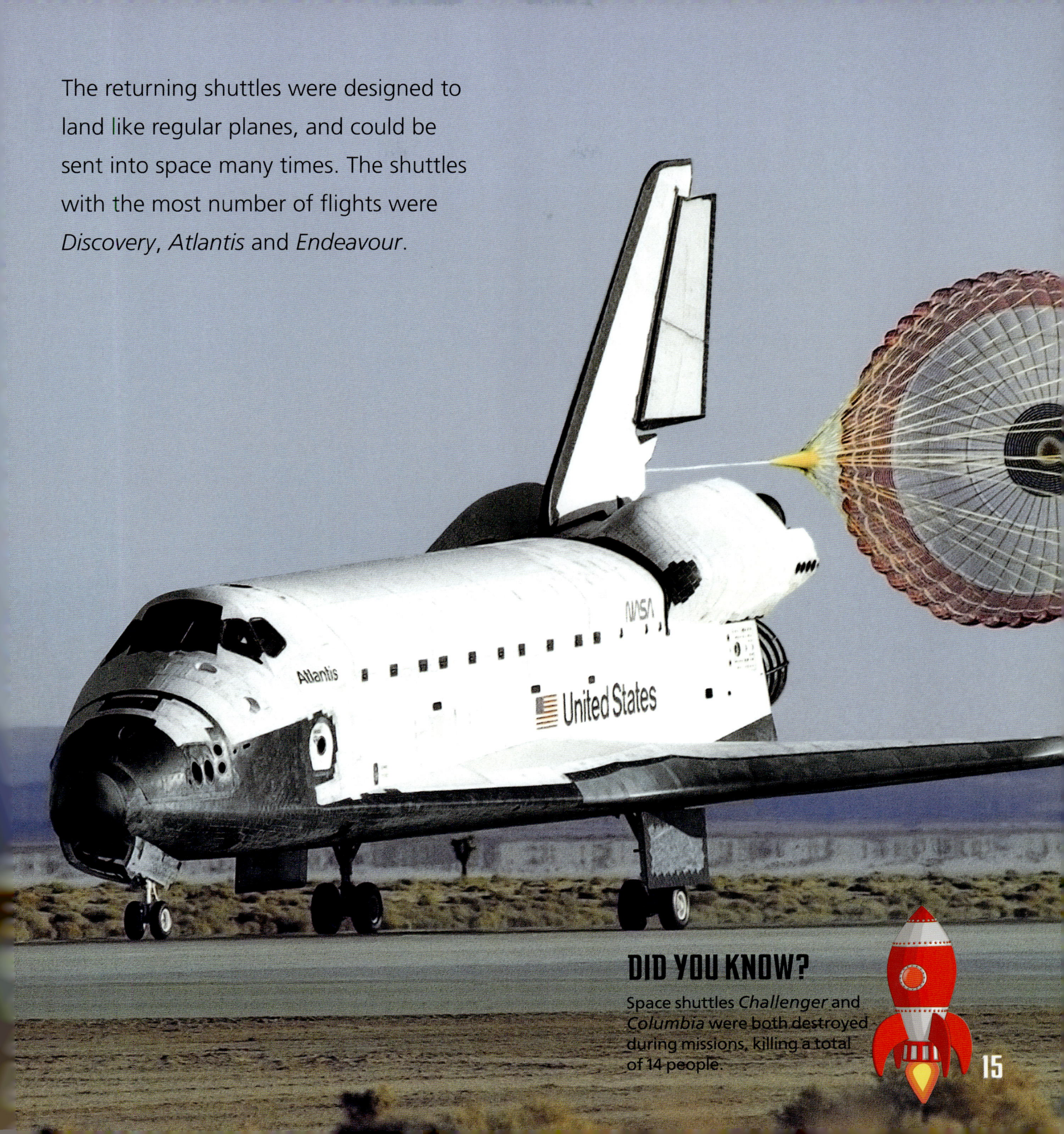

The returning shuttles were designed to land like regular planes, and could be sent into space many times. The shuttles with the most number of flights were *Discovery*, *Atlantis* and *Endeavour*.

DID YOU KNOW?
Space shuttles *Challenger* and *Columbia* were both destroyed during missions, killing a total of 14 people.

LIVING IN SPACE

A space station is a satellite that orbits the Earth. Small teams of astronauts live inside them, usually for less than a year at a time. Space stations are used for scientific experiments and to learn about the effects of long-term space travel on the human body.

DID YOU KNOW?

The longest amount of time a person has continuously lived in space is 438 days. This was achieved by Russian cosmonaut Valeri Polyakov, on the *Mir* space station.

The first space station launched into space was *Salyut 1*, by the Soviet Union in 1971. Other major space stations since then include NASA's *Skylab* and Russia's *Mir*. There are currently two space stations in orbit: the *International Space Station* and China's *Tiangong 1*.

ROVERS AND PROBES

Spacecraft that can operate without an astronaut on board are known as rovers or probes. Probes are designed to explore space and faraway planets, stars and galaxies, while rovers are designed to learn about planetary surfaces. The information these spacecraft collect is then sent back to Earth. *Cassini*, a probe launched by NASA in 1997, has sent incredible pictures taken from below Saturn's rings. The blue dot to the right is our home, planet Earth.

DID YOU KNOW?

The *Curiosity* rover, currently exploring Mars, is 3 metres long, 2.8 metres wide and 2 metres high. This is about the same size as a small car.

DEEP SPACE

Astronomers use unmanned spacecraft equipped with powerful telescopes to look at the farthest corners of space. This has helped scientists work out the age and size of the universe. The universe is calculated to be 13.8 billion years old.

DID YOU KNOW?

Our universe is home to hundreds of billions of galaxies. This spiral galaxy, known as Messier 74, contains around 100 billion stars.

SATELLITE COMMUNICATION

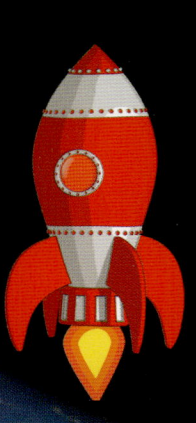

DID YOU KNOW?

There are more than 18,000 human-made objects orbiting the Earth. Close to 1,000 of these are working satellites, with the rest of these objects being classified as "space junk".

Satellites have come a long way since *Sputnik 1*. They have played and continue to play an important role in many of the technologies we use every day, such as television, radio, telephones and the internet. Communication satellites work by receiving information signals from one location on Earth, then sending the same information signals to another location on Earth. Before satellites this was very difficult or impossible to do over long distances.

First published in 2014 by
wild dog
54A Alexandra Parade
Clifton Hill Vic 3068
Australia
+61 3 9419 9406
dog@wdog.com.au
wdog.com.au

Copyright text © Eion Pty Ltd 2014
Copyright layout and design © Eion Pty Ltd 2014

All rights reserved. Apart from any fair dealing for the purpose of study, research, criticism or review, as permitted under the Copyright Act, no part of this book may be reproduced by any process, stored in a retrieval system, or transmitted in any form, without permission of the copyright owner. All enquiries should be made to the publisher at the address above.

Printed and bound by Everbest Printing Co. Ltd

FSC MIX Paper from responsible sources
FSC® C021256

FSC® is a non-profit international organisation established to promote the responsible management of the world's forests.

National Library of Australia Cataloguing-in-Publication data:
Author: Charles Hope, 1981.
Title: Space Exploration.
ISBN: 9781742033143 (pbk.)
Series: Going Supernova.
Target Audience: For primary school age.
Subjects: Outer space--Exploration--Juvenile literature.
Interplanetary voyages--Juvenile literature.
Supernovae--Juvenile literature.
Dewey Number: 387.8

PHOTO CREDITS:
Images courtesy of Shutterstock – Photographers: Front Cover Fer Gregory; p 1 Atypeek Design; p 2-3 manzrussali; p 4-5 Denis Tabler; p 8-9 Christian Kohler; p 18 Atypeek design; pp 20-21 Atypeek design; p 22-23 fongfong; pp 3, 5, 7, 9, 11, 13, 15, 17, 19, 21, 23 (rocket) Pie-Guy; p 24 AZP Worldwide; Back Cover iurii.

Images courtesy of NASA –
Pages 6, 7, 10, 11, 12, 13, 14, 15, 16-17, 19.

Wild Dog would like to thank Robert Barone-Nugent for his factual check of this book, and Neil Conning for his careful proofreading.

10 9 8 7 6 5 4 3 2   14 15 16 17 18

For more information on space exploration, check out the following NASA websites:
1) http://www.nasa.gov/audience/forkids/kidsclub/flash/#.UpbOtWT-LjI
2) http://www.nasa.gov/externalflash/nasacity/index2.htm

GLOSSARY:

ASTRONAUT: a person that is trained to travel in a spacecraft.
ASTRONOMERS: a person that studies the objects of space.
ATMOSPHERE: the gases that surround a particular planet.
BLACK HOLE: an area of space with an incredibly strong field of gravity.
CARGO: useful goods or products that are carried on board a spacecraft.
COSMONAUT: Russian word for astronaut.
MAGNIFY: to make something look bigger.
ORBIT: the path an object takes to travel around another object.
SATELLITE: a human-made or space object that orbits around another space object.
TELESCOPES: an instrument that makes distant objects look closer.
UNIVERSE: the entire contents of space.

INDEX:

Aldrin, Edwin "Buzz": 10, 11
Apollo 11: 10
Apollo program: 8-9, 12
Armstrong, Neil: 10
Atlantis: 15
Cassini: 18
Challenger: 15
Columbia: 15
Command module: 9
Curiosity: 19
Discovery: 15
Endeavour: 15
Gagarin, Yuri: 4
Galilei, Galileo: 3
Gemini Program: 8
Helms, Susan: 7
International Space Station: 14, 17
Leonov, Alexey: 6
Lunar module: 12
Lunar roving vehicle: 13
Mars: 19
Messier 74: 21
Mir: 17
NASA: 8, 17, 18
Netherlands: 3
Polyakov, Valeri: 17
Russia/Soviet Union: 4, 6, 17
Salyut 1: 17
Saturn: 18
Shepard, Alan: 4
Skylab: 17
Sputnik 1: 4, 23
Tiangong 1: 17
United States: 4
Voss, Jim: 7